"In And Beyond The Olive Sky"

A Poetry Collection of Love, Legacy, and the Lives Between Worlds

Divyaa Sood

India | USA | UK

Copyright © Divyaa Sood
All Rights Reserved.

This book has been self-published with all reasonable efforts taken to make the material error-free by the author. No part of this book shall be used, reproduced in any manner whatsoever without written permission from the author, except in the case of brief quotations embodied in critical articles and reviews.

The Author of this book is solely responsible and liable for its content including but not limited to the views, representations, descriptions, statements, information, opinions, and references ["Content"]. The Content of this book shall not constitute or be construed or deemed to reflect the opinion or expression of the Publisher or Editor. Neither the Publisher nor Editor endorse or approve the Content of this book or guarantee the reliability, accuracy, or completeness of the Content published herein and do not make any representations or warranties of any kind, express or implied, including but not limited to the implied warranties of merchantability, fitness for a particular purpose.

The Publisher and Editor shall not be liable whatsoever...

Made with ❤ on the BookLeaf Publishing Platform
www.bookleafpub.in
www.bookleafpub.com

Dedication

To my parents and my sister,
for being my roots when the world kept shifting.

To Ajay,
for teaching me that love can stand guard even under olive skies.

And to every soul,
who has ever waited, believed, and become - these pages are yours.

Preface

There are worlds we live in, and worlds we quietly build within.

As a Fauji wife, I've known both — the structured calm of olive days and the restless hum of waiting nights. But beyond those walls of duty and distance, there lies another world — the one of reflections, faith, healing, and hope.

In and Beyond the Olive Sky was born out of both — the seen and the unseen.

It's a collection of poems that travel through my seasons — of love and waiting, of strength and surrender, of loss and becoming. Some are drawn from the rhythm of the Fauji life, where time stands still and hearts march on. Others are whispers from my everyday — lessons that life keeps handing me in cups of tea, pauses, and prayers.

Each poem is a fragment of a larger journey — one that begins within the olive skies of duty and discipline, but dares to look beyond, into the infinite blue of becoming.

This is my heart — uniformed and unguarded.

— Divyaa Sood

Acknowledgements

First, to my parents, whose unwavering love, guidance, and quiet sacrifices shaped the woman I am today. Every lesson, every hug, every word of encouragement lives within these pages.

To my sister, my lifelong companion and confidante, who laughed with me, cried with me, and held my hand through every twist and turn — this book carries fragments of our shared memories and unspoken understandings.

To Ajay, whose courage in uniform, patience, and steadfast presence have anchored my heart and inspired my words — this book is a testament to the love and strength we share across distance and time.

To every Fauji wife who knows the art of waiting with grace, the weight of silent strength, and the quiet victories behind every goodbye — your stories breathe through these poems.

To my readers, past, present, and future — may these verses remind you that life is a tapestry of ordinary days and extraordinary moments, and that love, patience, and reflection are what carry us beyond the skies we inhabit.

And finally, **to the sky above, olive and infinite**, for reminding me that no matter where we are, there is always room to soar.

— Divyaa Sood

1.. "My First Salute To The Fauji Life"

I stepped from civil streets so known,
Into a world not quiet my own,
Devlali called, my very first place,
With uniforms, bugles and measured grace.

My husband, buried in books and drills,
While I climbed unseen, untested hills,
A course of life my mother's hand,
Could never teach or help me stand.

For this was a world with unspoken codes,
Of saree pleats and mess-night modes,
Of letters carried, of phones delayed,
Of silent strength, not ready–made.

At first, I flattered, unsure, unseen,
This olive world was crisp, pristine,
But hands reached out, both kind and wise,
From ladies with battle in their eyes.

They showed me how to walk the line,
To hold my own light, to shine.
They taught me warmth, they taught me cheer,
To blend my voice, yet still be clear.

We laughed in rooms in echoing walls,
We cried at sudden midnight calls,
We built a bond so rare, so true,
A sisterhood that pulled me through.

Yes, life had losses, sharp and deep,
Memories that still make me grieve,
But every pain carved out a space,
For courage, love and lasting grace.

So, I paved my way, step after stride,
With friends as compass, heart as guide,
And in this Fauji life I see,
The woman I was meant to be.

2. "In His Eyes, I Am Everything"

He looks at me,
Like the stars would stop shining - If I ever closed my eyes.
Like his day doesn't begin until I smile – and ends when I do.

In his world, I am not background noise.
I am the song, the meaning,
The only reason he turns the page.

He knows the sound of my silence,
The way I fidget when I am scared.
How I like my coffee, and where I hide my tears.

He speaks in ways, no one else can hear-
With hands that hold gently,
And eyes that say, "You are my home."

It's not obsession, Its devotion,

It's love that doesn't need to be chased.
Because it never runs.

In his presence, I forget I was ever ensure-
Because when he looks at me,
I see a woman worth the universe.

And to him I am the calm, after the storms.
The dreams he never dares to - wake from.
Not the piece of his life- but the whole picture.

He doesn't promise the moon-
He brings it to me,
Wrapped in patience, sealed with truth.

And if this is love- the kind that stays,
That softens without breaking,
That builds without burning-

Then let it be forever, because in his eyes,
I am everything, and with him,
I finally believe it too.

3. "The Rush I Waited For"

I waited so long, with hope wearing thin,
Each day felt a battle, I could not win.
Dreams slipped away like sand through my hands,
I wondered if joy would ever still stand.

I almost gave up, I almost let go,
The fire inside has burned too low.
The night felt endless, the mornings the same,
Life was a circle, a tiresome game.

But then it happened – sudden, so fast,
Like the first breath of spring after winter has passed.
My heart beat wild, my blood ran high,
I felt I could run, I felt I could fly.

The moment I prayed for, the one I denied,
Came rushing to me like waves to the tide.
I laughed, I cried, I stood in surprise,
The world look new through my shinny eyes.

All those years of waiting, of carrying pain,
Were worth every tear, every heavy chain.
For happiness strikes when you least expect,
A gift from the storm, a joy to protect.

I learned one truth and I'll keep it near –
The wait may be long, but the rush is clear.
Don't quit on your heart when the journey is tough,
Sometimes the waiting is what makes it enough.

4. "Belonging To The Regiment"

Student days were left behind,
Books and drills, a disciplined grind.
Now came the call, the soldiers test-
To join the unit to know the rest.

I had seen his sweat, his fight, his pain,
The sleepless nights, the endless strain.
But this was different, a deeper fire,
The regimental spirit, the heart's desire.

With cautious steps, I crossed the gate,
A world unknown, yet carved my fate.
Would I be seen, would I belong?
Or fade away in a crowd so strong?

In my late twenties still so young,
Dreams half – bloomed, song unsung,
And then – like playful, sudden spree,
A voice called out, "Aunty!" – to me.

I smiled at first, then paused in thought,
A new respect that moment brought.
For in that word, though strange, so true,
Lay trust, acceptance, something new.

The mess stood tall the stories untold,
Of Rajput valour, fierce and bold.
I watched the banners, the shinning crest,
And felt my heart beat match their chest.

The dining – in – my very first,
My nerves like clouds about to burst.
But laughter rang and kindness poured,
Like old friends seated around a board.

Each toast was raised with fire and pride,
Each tale of courage, nothing to hide.
I felt a strength, both fierce and kind,
A family formed, both soul and mind.

The doubts I carried, quiet, unsure,
Melted away – I needed no cure.
For here I was, not guest, not child,
But one of their own, embraced beguiled.

I saw in their eyes a truth so bright,

That love and duty walk in light.
That wives too wear an unseen crest,
Guardians of courage, silently dressed.

And slowly, softly, it came to me,
This is my world, where I meant to be.
Not just his shadow, not just his pride,
But a Rajput's wife, with a clan beside.

So, let the bugle call, let the flags all wave,
This bond is sacred, steadfast, brave,
For in that welcome, I truly knew,
The regiment's heart beats in me too.

5. "The Dreams We Call Forward"

A spark begins inside the heart,
A quiet thought, a tiny start.
It whispers soft, it dares to grow,
A seed of power you already know.

Close your eyes, see it clear,
Hold it close, draw it near.
The mind's a magnet, strong and wide,
It pulls the world to what's inside.

Speak your wish, let it fly,
Don't ask how, don't ask why.
The wind will carry, stars will guide,
What you believe can't be denied.

Action, steps, though small, must show,
Each one builds, the river flows.
Faith is fuel, and trust the flame,
Your dream arrives when you call its name.

Remember this: the world's a mirror,
Your truth reflects, the path grows clearer.
Gratitude open unseen doors,
The more you thank, the more you pour.

So, stand up tall, command your space,
Lift your voice with steady grace.
Manifest with soul and might,
Turn your darkness into light.

No wish too bold, no prayer too far,
Your soul was born to chase the stars.
Believe, receive, let courage steer,
The dream you call is already here.

6. "Two Sides of One Sky"

A smile to me may heal the day,
To you it might feel far away.
A gentle word can sound like gold,
Or cut too sharp, too harsh, too cold.

The rain that makes my spirit sing,
May weigh you down, a heavy thing.
The light that guides my steps at night,
Might blind your eyes, too sharp, too bright.

The song I hum may ease my pain,
For you it stirs old wounds again.
The silence, I call deep and kind,
Might press too heavy on your mind.

The fire that wears my trembling hand,
May scorch the dreams you try to stand.
The shield I hold to guard my soul,
Might block your way, might take its toll.

What lifts my heart may bend your own,
What feels like seed to me, to you, its stone.
What gives me wings may clip your flight,
What's warm to me may burn your sight.

The truth I tell may sound like care,
But strike you raw, too sharp to bear.
The prayer I breath may give me rest,
But weigh as doubt upon your chest.

The gift I gave, may feel like chains,
The joy I share, may spark your pains.
The choice I make, may set me free,
Yet feel like loss when seen by thee.

So, here's the truth we learn to hold:
Two thoughts, one talk, yet stories told.
It's not to harm, nor to defend,
But walk with care, and hearts will mend.

The sky is wide, for both, for all,
One sun may rise, and yet shadows fall.
Live with the balance, give and take –
Two sides of one sky, the same path we make.

7. "Sisterhood In Olive Hues"

We gather not in rank or file,
But hearts that march the extra mile.
Through whispered hopes and midnight tea,
We share a bond — unspoken, free.

While duty calls our men away,
We hold the fort, come what may.
From power cuts to posting blues,
We paint our lives in olive hues.

We laugh through moves, through packs and tears,
We toast to love, outlast the fears.
Our sarees sway, our spirits bloom,
We turn each house into soulful perfume.

Each "goodbye" makes our courage grow,
Each "hello" warms the hearts we know.
We trade our roots for borrowed skies,
Yet never lose our bright goodbyes.

Not every woman can take this road,
To wear the strength, bear the load.
It takes more than charm, more than pride,
To stand alone while worlds collide.

We mend the sink, we soothe the child,
We guard our dreams — both meek and wild.
We learn to laugh, though hearts may break,
To stand in calm when storms awake.

Some nights are long, and tears run deep,
Some mornings cold, yet chores to keep.
We hold the home when ranks march far,
And cradle hope like a northern star.

We speak in glances, we share our fears,
We weave our stories through the years.
Our sisterhood, a quiet might,
A gentle blaze in the darkest night.

We learn to bend, to stretch, to sway,
To find our peace when skies are grey.
We rise, we fall, we rise again,
With laughter sharp as soldier's pain.

For while they serve the nation's call,

We serve in silence, giving all.
We may not wear the stripes they do,
But we shine — loyal, fierce, and true.

We are the calm behind the storm,
The unseen courage, quiet, warm.
Not every heart can take this fight,
But we — we shine through endless night.

So, here's to us — this chosen tribe,
Who live with strength, with joy, with vibe.
We anchor love, we break, we bind,
We are the sisters – we leave no one behind.

8. "The Question Of Us"

They say we're the crown of the earth,
The flame of spirit, the gift of birth.
Hands that build, and hearts that dream,
Minds that shape the grandest scheme.

We touched the stars, we tamed the skies,
We learned to question, reason, ask "why."
With fire and stone, with wheel and light,
We turned the dark into endless night.

But see the rivers, choked and dry,
Forests falling, creatures cry.
The oceans boil, the mountains weep,
The graves we have dug are far too deep.

We speak of kindness, yet sharpen blades,
Build towers tall while conscience fades.
We swear by love, but live by greed,
Take more than ever we truly need.

Children laugh, then bombs thrown,
Cities burn while seed are sown.
We heal with science, yet spread disease,
We preach of truth, yet twist with ease.

Are we the miracle God once planned,
Or just the shadow that stains the land?
Are we the poem carved in clay,
Or scribbles fading fast away?

Still, hope flickers – a gentle flame,
Each small act done in mercy's name.
When we forgive, when we embrace,
A bit of heavens lights this place.

So, humankind: the curse, the cure,
The best, the worst, none can be sure.
Perhaps the test is just to strive,
To make this fleeting gift alive.

So, tell me reader, plain and true,
What's your answer – me or you?
Are we worth this life we're living,
Or just wasting the gift we were given?

9. "The Empty Chair"

I reach for you, but find the air,
A voice now gone, an empty chair.
The room still holds your gentle trace,
But time has swept away your face.

We laughed, we fought, we shared the days,
In little talks, in quiet ways.
And now the silence speaks so loud,
A heavy cloak, a grieving shroud.

The deals of life are hard and true,
It gave me love, then asked for you.
No bargain to struck, no choice to make,
Just sudden loss, a heart to break.

The nights are long, the memory cold,
The stories left remain untold.
I search the sky, I walk the ground,
Hoping for signs where none are found.

Yet in my chest, though torn, though scarred,
I keep you safe, though keeping's hard.
For love does not just end, it stays,
It threads through dark, it lights my days.

And though I grieve the space you've left,
Though memory feels sharp bereft.
Your laughter still, your kindness near,
Reminds me love is stronger here.

So, loss may cut, and tears may fall,
But love outlines the grave, the wall.
The chair is empty, yet I know,
You walk beside me as I go.

10. "When Destiny Ordered Coffee"
(A Love Written Beneath the Olive Sky)

It didn't begin in candlelight,
Nor promises whispered through the night.
Just a wedding, some laughter, a friendly face,
And fate deciding to quicken its pace.

Two aunties plotting — as aunties do,
"Let's match them up, they'll make it through."
A call was made, a spark took flight,
And your voice slipped softly into my night.

We spoke for weeks — no plans, no claim,
Just jokes, confessions, and quiet flame.
A month of words, of "what if" and "when,"
Till duty bowed, and you said, "I'll come then."

Barista, Sector Thirty-Five — that's where,
The air smelled of mocha and a nervous flair.
Two cups of coffee, a silent test,
Two strangers trying to give their best.

We smiled, we fumbled, we looked away,
Small talk danced and lost its way.
But something deeper hummed inside,
Like a tide we both refused to hide.

"Okay, bye," we said, polite, unsure,
But destiny laughed — it had more in store.
"Let's watch a movie?" — casual, sly,
And Burfi became our alibi.

Popcorn, laughter, the screen glow,
Two quiet hearts beginning to know.
I dropped you home — no words, no plea,
But my heart whispered, "He's the one for me."

Weeks later, fate played its twist,
The kind you almost can't resist.
Old albums opened, memories spun —
"Wait, you were there? You were the one!"

Same school benches, same playground skies,
From nursery smiles to second-grade eyes.

Two tiny souls in the same small hall,
Who never knew their future call.

Years went by, paths went wide,
Till life looped back to set it right.
From crayons to coffee, what a flight —
Destiny doesn't rush, but oh, it writes.

Now olive hues paint our sky,
With laughter, love, and reasons why.
From "hello" calls to "take care" texts,
To vows unspoken, to what came next.

No lightning struck, no love cliché,
Just peace that said, "You're home to stay."
Because love's not loud — it's soft, it's shy,
Like that day… when destiny ordered coffee — you and I.

"When Destiny Ordered Coffee"
Because some stories don't start with fireworks —
They start with childhood, distance, and one perfect cup.

11. "When Doors Don't Close, The Soul Erodes"

A closure is a gentle key,
It sets the restless spirit free.
It ties the knots, it seals the seam,
And gives the weary heart a dream.

Without its turn, the shadows stay,
They steal your light, they block your way.
A wound unhealed, a song unsung,
Will weigh you down, keep chains unstrung.

Unfinished words, unanswered cries,
Will chain your heart, will cloud your skies.
Peace won't bloom where silence grows,
It lingers long, it never goes.

The mind replays, the soul still yearns,
For doors to shut, for tides to turn.
But if denied that scared close,
The pain will linger, sharp as prose.

To close a door is not the end,
It teaches time the way to mend.
It's saying softly, this is done,
So, healing's work can begin.

But left ajar, the echoes rise,
They haunt your nights, they stain your skies.
And every step feels tied to then,
Till peace deserts the soul again.

So, grant the end its rightful place,
To clear the storm, to cleanse the space.
For without closure the pain remains,
A ghost that drags in unseen chains.

Closure is love's last gentle grace,
A final bow, a soft embrace.
It doesn't kill what came before,
It guards the soul, it shuts the door.

12. "The In Between"

Not the dawn, not the night,
Not the flame, not the ash.
A hush between the wrong and right,
A mirror cracked, a shattered glass.

It is a place where footsteps slow,
Where questions bloom, but answers hide.
Where hearts half – empty, half – aflow,
Still ache, but keep a quiet pride.

The In Between is neither rest,
Nor running hard towards fire.
It is the weary, fragile chest,
That holds the ghost of old desire.

Not failing fully, not yet tall,
Not saying nothing, not saying all.
The tongue is tied, the breath is thin,
And yet the soul keeps stirring within.

It smells of rain that never came,
It feels of hope that lost its name.
It wears the weight of half – spun years,
It drinks the salt of hidden tears.

The In Between is not a place –
It's how heart forgets it's pace.
A half – closed eyes, a half – said prayer,
A silence heavy in the air.

Here giving up feels near at hand,
And yet the knees refuse to land.
Here hope is not a golden ray,
But faint smoke drifting, gone away.

And yet, inside this shadowed space,
Something unseen begins to trace.
A spark too small to call it light,
But still, it keeps the dark in sight.

For every soul that's lost its way,
Has lingered here, has had to stay.
Between the breaking and the mend,
Between the pause and what may bend.

The In Between – this middle ground,
Where neither silence nor song is found.

Where weary heart, though torn, still lean,
On what it means – to be unseen.

13. "Now I Know What It Meant To Be Them"
The Quiet Inheretance Of Love and Strength

I grew up soft beneath their shade,
Unaware of what foundations they laid.
The world felt kind, the skies were clear,
Because they hid the storms from near.

There was no hunger, no borrowed grace,
Just gentle love and a steady place.
Two daughters, bright and endlessly free —
Yet never once did they let us see—

The weight of whispers, sharp and thin,
That called two girls a lesser win.
They smiled through it all, fierce and proud,
Defying the noise, standing unbowed.

I never saw their tired eyes,
The small goodbyes in each compromise.
They never sighed, they never said,
How heavy dreams can feel as bread.

I argued once, as children do,
Believing they just never knew.
That freedom meant a wilder call,
That parents simply built the wall.

But now I stand where they once stood,
Balancing chaos, life, and good.
And suddenly the view has changed —
The heart rearranged, the roles exchanged.

I see the calm they had to fake,
The sleepless nights for my own sake.
How every "no" was made with care,
And every silence whispered prayer.

They made it look like ease and grace,
Like love was light, with no dark place.
But I now know — it took a toll,
To give their hearts and still stay whole.

They failed sometimes, but not for long,
They turned their faults to gentle song.

They laughed through loss, they danced through pain,
So, I'd just see the joy remain.

And now, when I hold my child so tight,
In quiet hours before the light,
I feel their echo, deep and true —
Their patience living in what I do.

I never thanked them quite enough,
For teaching love without the tough.
For showing pride where fear could bloom,
And filling silence with endless room.

Now I know what it meant to be them —
The ones who fought, but never condemned.
Who made each struggle seem like art,
And loved me with their whole brave heart.

14. "The Missing Key To Happiness"

I looked in drawers of self-help books,
In mirrors lined with practiced looks.
In filtered smiles and scattered feeds –
All places where joy plants its seeds.

I asked the gurus, tall and tanned,
Who sold me peace with polished brand.
I drank their tea, I said their chants,
But still felt off in yoga pants.

I chased success and ticked each box,
Tried morning walks and mindful talks.
I set big goals and get things done,
But still felt empty, even won.

Where was this key, this magic spark?
Was it lost in some realm too dark?
Was it buried in blissful goodbyes?
Or packed in tears I let run dry?

And then one night, tea cold – hair wild,
I laughed alone, just like a child.
No make up mask, no need to post,
Just me, unfiltered, burnt toast.

And there it was – not loud, not grand,
No marching band or holding hand.
Just a soft, breath, a blink, a beat,
A moment where my heart felt – complete.

Turns out the key's not gold or new,
It's chipped, its quiet, sometimes you knew.
It's held in hands that make your tea,
In being weird, in feeling free.

So, If you have lost it – join the crowd,
It hides in places not allowed.
By Pinterest boards or TED x talks –
It lives in messy, barefoot walks.

Not something bought or planned or pressed –
The key to joy is a little rest.
A little grace, a plate half – full,
A life that's strange yet beautiful.

15. "The Woman Beneath The Olive Sky"

She was born of dawn and dust and dreams,
Her laughter like rivers, her hope in streams.
A girl who painted stars with her sigh,
Long before she lived beneath the olive sky.

She dreamt of cities, of velvet light,
Of ink-stained fingers, and words that ignite.
Of paths unpaved and songs unsung,
Of stories whispered and battles won.

But fate — that wily general — drew her near,
To a man whose courage conquered fear.
In his eyes, she saw the nation's call,
In his voice, she heard the bugle's thrall.

And love — that timeless uniform —
Wrapped her soul in a sacred form.
He marched ahead, she stood behind,
Yet both were one — in heart and mind.

Now she walks where the olive winds sigh,
Her dreams tucked gently in the sky.
Each dawn, a letter, each dusk, a prayer,
Each breath, a promise she learns to bear.

A Fauji wife — not just a name,
But a quiet badge of love and flame.
Her strength isn't thunder, it's the rain,
That falls unseen yet heals the pain.

She wears her grace like a medal of gold,
With stories untold and hearts grown bold.
The world sees calm; she hides the storm,
Duty and dignity her chosen form.

When the bugles sound and flags arise,
She looks up to those olive skies.
He salutes the nation — she salutes fate,
Each goodbye echoing, "Stand tall. Wait."

In laughter borrowed, in tears concealed,
Her courage blooms on the battlefield.
For she too serves — unseen, unsaid,
In every sleepless night she's bled.

Her letters are lullabies laced with pride,

Her faith the anchor where storms collide.
While he guards borders wide and high,
She guards his world beneath the sky.

She is the silence behind the cheer,
The whispered strength the brave hold dear.
The world may never hear her cry,
Yet her courage hums through the olive sky.

The girl within her still dreams bright,
Of stardust, poems, and city light.
But she has learned — the truest flight,
Is finding peace in endless night.

For she is not lost — she's redefined,
A woman of fire, of faith, of mind.
Her aura glows — quiet, yet high,
The eternal woman beneath the olive sky.

16. "The Keeper Of My Chaos"
(She Knows My Secrets.... and Still Calls Me Sister)

From scraped knees to grown-up sighs,
From stolen sweets to made-up lies,
You've kept my secrets, one by one,
While I blabbed yours just for fun.

I am selfish, you are not,
Yet you've borne me—tantrums and thought.
You've been the balm to soothe my doubt,
Even when I've ratted you out!

You used to pinch my school bag tight,
Each morning, turning chaos to light.
We'd jump and giggle on the road as stray,
Like two mad souls who'd lost their way.

Because in my mind, I had a thought—
"You're elder, so you handle the lot."
I left my worries, small and few,
All dumped (politely) on you.

But now I see, you needed too,
An elder one to lean into.
I wish I'd known back then to say,
"I care for you in my silly way."

You've been my diary without a page,
My calm, my cure, my comic stage.
When I spilled juice on Mom's new chair,
You took the blame (why?!)—unfair!

You knew my crushes, my fears, my schemes,
You saved me from my wildest dreams.
When I ruined your dress or hid your shoe,
You sighed, "She's mine... what can I do?"

I broke your stuff, I stole your snacks,
Copied your homework behind your backs.
Yet when the world got cold and grim,
You pulled me close and said, "Sink or swim."

You're the reason my chaos stays contained,
My storm half-tamed, my guilt unchained.

You're the secret I can never hide,
My crime partner and my guide.

And though I tattled, teased, and pried,
You still walk proudly by my side.
You're the wisdom in my wild,
The adult who forgives the child.

We are two souls, one crazy blend,
A war, a peace, that'll never end.
Darkest secret, brightest star—
You've seen me worse, and loved me far.

So here's to the sister who never told,
Who kept my chaos wrapped in gold.
If loyalty had a name, I'd say—
It's you, my secret keeper... come what may.

17. "Chatter's Gold" (How lies Go Shopping... and Truth gets Trampled)

Oh, rumours, sweet little merchants of air,
They travel fast, without a care.
A wink, a nod, a "did you hear?"
And suddenly facts disappear.

They ride on tongues like luxury cars,
Faster than reason, outpacing stars.
From kitchen whispers to boardroom cheers,
They feast on worry, gossip, fears.

The teller smiles, so innocent, so sly,
"Oh, I just heard..." — while truths go die.
They sprinkle drama, garnish it neat,
And serve it hot on every street.

Who profits most from this sly parade?
Not the truth, which is poorly paid.

You're the secret I can never hide,
My crime partner and my guide.

And though I tattled, teased, and pried,
You still walk proudly by my side.
You're the wisdom in my wild,
The adult who forgives the child.

We are two souls, one crazy blend,
A war, a peace, that'll never end.
Darkest secret, brightest star—
You've seen me worse, and loved me far.

So here's to the sister who never told,
Who kept my chaos wrapped in gold.
If loyalty had a name, I'd say—
It's you, my secret keeper... come what may.

17. "Chatter's Gold"
(How lies Go Shopping...
and Truth gets Trampled)

Oh, rumours, sweet little merchants of air,
They travel fast, without a care.
A wink, a nod, a "did you hear?"
And suddenly facts disappear.

They ride on tongues like luxury cars,
Faster than reason, outpacing stars.
From kitchen whispers to boardroom cheers,
They feast on worry, gossip, fears.

The teller smiles, so innocent, so sly,
"Oh, I just heard..." — while truths go die.
They sprinkle drama, garnish it neat,
And serve it hot on every street.

Who profits most from this sly parade?
Not the truth, which is poorly paid.

It's the schemers, the smug, the sly,
The ones who watch while others cry.

"Oh, really?" we gasp, wide-eyed, aghast,
Not knowing the tale will never last.
Yet we sip it like fine champagne,
Unaware it carries hidden pain.

Rumours are currency, shiny, bright,
Traded in shadows, hidden from light.
They buy attention, status, and fame,
While honest hearts are stuck with shame.

Some spread it for fun, a laugh, a tease,
Some sell it quietly, like stocks with ease.
The clever grin, the sly head tilt,
While everyone else wears guilt like quilt.

Oh, how we chase this sparkling lie,
Passing it on as if it's wise.
We trade in whispers, we traffic in hearsay,
And feed the beast that dances our way.

Truth trudges, slow and heavy-footed,
Rumour races, sharp and saluted.
It bends, it twists, it grows, it mocks,
Turns simple words into ticking clocks.

So next time a whisper brushes your ear,
Ask whose hands are wiping their tear.
Who's laughing behind the curtained wall,
While you stumble, trip, and fall?

Yes, gossip is golden — at least for some,
For those who weave, and never succumb.
But beware the glitter, the sparkling bait,
Rumour's joy is your unwitting fate.

18. "The Measure Beyond Might"
(An Ode To The Making Of A Gentleman)

A man is born of muscle and flame,
Of restless dreams and thirst for name.
He builds his walls, he claims his land,
Yet gentleness slips through his hand.

For manhood starts in blood and bone,
But greatness blooms when pride has flown.
A gentleman is not by birth,
He's carved by conscience, proof of worth.

A man may roar to prove he's loud,
A gentleman need not please the crowd.
He rules no hearts with fear or show,
His quiet strength compels them so.

He does not wear his wounds as fame,
He heals the hurt and asks no name.
He listens long, he speaks with care,
He fights for peace, yet honours fair.

A man may guard what he can hold,
A gentleman guards hearts, not gold.
He leads not just by might or plan,
He leads by being more than man.

He lifts, he steadies, learns to yield,
His courage blooms in mercy's field.
He bows to none but truth and grace,
And leaves compassion in his place.

But now — the times have lost their hue,
The rare, the kind, the good, the true.
Gentlemen have grown so few,
We tell our women, "Man up" too.

What irony, what loss, what shame,
That gentleness became a game.
We crown the loud, we cheer the bold,
But kindness now feels quaint, or old.

So ask yourself — what will you be?
A shadow, or integrity?

A man of might, of fleeting fame,
Or one who earns a gentler name?

All men are born beneath the sun,
But few evolve when day is done.
It takes far more than strength or plan —
To rise, to fall...
To be a man.

For every boy can stand and shout,
But few can calm their storms without.
It takes rare courage, deep and true,
To choose restraint — to start anew.

So, choose your path, and choose it well,
The tale you leave, the truth you tell.
For manhood's common, easy, free —
But gentleman is mastery.

19. "The Man I Love, The Soldier I Stand Beside"

He rises before the dawn, the world still in dreams,
  The man I love with quiet streams.
  At home, his laugh warms every space,
    Yet duty paints a different face.

The soldier walks, the armour goes on,
A steadfast heart to greet the dawn.
For the nation calls, its needs are high.
And he answers without question, without sigh.

But I see the man beneath the steel,
  The tender soul, the love I feel.
His inner child still whispers, still dreams,
Yet he balances life on impossible beams.

Each mission he takes, each post he defends,
  Becomes a story where family bends.
  Our longing waits in every night,
  Yet pride blooms in the nation's light.

Sometimes I see him torn and small,
Between the man, the child, the call.
He fights for us, for what's right and true,
And still finds ways to love me too.

The man I love is quiet and deep,
The soldier brave, the promises keep.
Two souls within one body reside,
One for the nation, one by my side.

When letters arrive, I see his care,
In every word, a love so rare.
His purpose stretches far and wide,
Yet every heart beat keeps me inside.

And though the world may never see,
How he battles for all that will be.
I stand in awe, I stand in pride,
The man I love, the soldier I walk beside.

He sacrifices, yet laughter says,
In fleeting moments, in stolen days.
A hero's heart, a love's glance,
In both, our lives find their dance.

So, I hold his hand, I share his skies,

The soldier's truth, the man's eyes.
For love is strong and love survives,
Even when the world tests our lives.

The man I love, the soldier I see,
Is both for the nation, yet belongs to me.
A sacred balance, a quiet song,
In his strength, I find where I belong.

20. "The Sacred Thread Of Promise"
(An Ode to the Soul's Vow)

A promise is not spoken – it's born,
Not crafted by lips, but by the dawn.
That rises after the storm's last cry,
By the hush of hope that refuses to die.

It is the breath between two souls,
Invisible, yet it binds the wholes.
No temple stone, no written creed,
Holds the power of one true deed.

A promise is the sacred thread unseen,
Stitched through the spaces where hearts have been.
It hums beneath every vow and prayer,
The truth that lingers in silent air.

It is life's mirror – clear unkind,
Reflecting the depth of a faithful mind.

It doesn't fade when seasons change,
It bends, it breaks – yet still remains.

A promise is not weak – it bleeds,
It fights, it endures, it plants new seeds.
It is the courage to stay, not flee,
The will to be what we swore to be.

When time unravels all, we've known,
And faces fade, and hearts have flown.,
A promise stands – calm, austere,
The sentinel of all we hold dear.

It's the prayer of lovers, the oath of kin,
The bridge where forgiveness begins.
It's not perfection, it's the climb,
The mark we leave beyond our time.

A promise is not tongue's delight,
It's the battle between wrong and right.
It's the tear unshed, the word unsaid,
The truth we live when all else is dead.

So, don't make promises you cannot keep,
For some hearts are wounded far too deep.
Don't let your words make others weak,
Your vow might be the hope they seek.

For you may never truly know,
How one kind word helps courage grow.
For life itself is a promise – pure divine,
A fleeting breath of grand design.

So, guard your promises – pure and kind,
Let love and truth be intertwined.
When all else break, when world forgets your name,
Your promise will still burn – like a flame.

21. "Mind vs. Heart: The Unending Debate"

My heart writes poems; my mind edits lines,
My soul hums quietly between the signs.
It's chaos here—no ringmaster in sight,
Just truth and trembling locked in fight.

The heart says, "Leap!"; the mind says, "Wait!",
The soul sighs softly, "Both are fate."
The heart wants thunder, wants rain and song,
The mind keeps asking, "What if it's wrong?"

My heart keeps bleeding ink and flame,
My mind turns passion into name and shame.
The heart runs barefoot through fields of fire,
The mind wears armour—built from desire.

The heart says, "Love, even if it burns!"
The mind says, "Learn—before the world turns."
The soul just laughs, half-ash, half-light,
And whispers, "You both make the night too bright."

Some days, I'm reason dressed as grace,
Some days, emotion paints my face.
They pull me apart, they tear, they mend—
And I call it living, again and again.

The heart is chaos, the mind, control,
But the soul—ah, the soul—is the quiet patrol.
It guards the ruins these two have made,
It waters the roots of what won't fade.

The heart forgives what logic condemns,
The mind defends where feeling bends.
The soul just stands—like a sacred tree,
Whispering, "War is what sets you free."

I've lost to both and won with none,
Yet somehow, that's how growth is done.
For peace isn't silence, it's this debate—
Between what we love and what we wait.

So, let them fight till stars are dust,
Till dreams decay and bones turn rust.
For the mind may rule, the heart may plead—
But the soul decides what I truly need.

22. "The Phoenix Path" (A Journey Of Rise and Redemption)

In lands where twilight hides the sky,
I walked alone, no wings to fly.
A heart once lost, a kingdom gone,
Where shadows lingered all day long.

I carried scars from choices made,
Bridges burned and trust betrayed.
The ground I walked felt cold and rough,
Every step was hard enough.

A storm came roaring, fierce and wild,
It shook my soul, it scared the child
Who once believed in brighter days,
Now lost inside a smoky haze.

But far away, a soft bell rang,
A tiny light, a hopeful clang.

It called me forward, made me rise,
To face the truth, to see the skies.

I met the ghosts that haunted me,
Each one a shadow I had to see.
I fought my fear, I climbed each hill,
With steady heart and iron will.

Through dark forests and rivers wide,
Through nights of grief where demons hide,
I found a spark, so small, so true,
A flame of hope to carry through.

The battles raged, but I grew strong,
Each struggle taught where I belong.
Forgiveness earned, not freely given,
My soul reborn, my spirit risen.

I climbed the cliffs of my despair,
Felt winds of change move through my hair.
The storm grew calm, the sky grew clear,
A new world opened, bright and near.

No longer captive, no longer chained,
I seized the dawn, my heart unfeigned.
Each step a song, each breath a cheer,
The Phoenix rises, the path is clear.

Redemption is not soft or brief,
It's a journey through pain and grief.
A story told through loss and gain,
Through tears, through fire, through every strain.

Now here I stand, a soul refined,
A path once dark, now brightly lined.
From shadow deep to radiant day,
Through trials faced, I found my way.

23. "The Stillness Of Mind - Truest Flow Of Life"

In alleys of endless running,
Breath grows tired, stumbling, stunning.
Dreams unfinished, worries loud,
Heartbeat scattered in the crowd.

Then a voice within does say –
"Pause, O mind, just drift away.
Be the lake, so calm, so deep,
Leave the noise, the restless leap."

The sunbeam whispers soft and bright,
"True light shines, in quiet height.
Upon the peak it sits and gleams,
Reflecting back its silent dreams."

The winds declare – though ever in flight,
Power is born in moments of quiet.
The waves may race through ocean wide,
But peace is found at the shore's side.

When the rivers thought slows down,
An inner nectar flows around.
When the world is hushed, unmoving,
The soul's own hymn is gently proving.

Stillness is no lifeless end,
It is the truth the path, the friend.
To walk, then stop, to breath, to hear,
That is life's meaning, pure and clear.

A flower blooms – its fragrance stays,
A word is spoken – it lights the way.
But when the mind in stillness lies,
The soul sings truths that never dies.

24. "The Olive Playground: Ballads Of The Fauji Kids"

We were born where flags salute the dawn,
Where boots march on and fathers are gone.
Where mothers wear courage like their grace,
And silence whispers in every base.

Our lullabies were sirens' cries,
Our night-lamps were the border skies.
We learnt to laugh with half a heart,
For every hug had a countdown start.

We shifted homes like shifting sands,
New friends, new schools, new trembling hands.
Yet somehow, in that restless air,
We found our roots everywhere.

Our playgrounds echoed with bugle calls,
Our medals hung on barrack walls.
We played with dreams, not just with toys—
Daughters fierce, and lionhearted boys.

We learnt to run before we crawled,
To hide our tears when duty called.
Our birthdays came with absent seats,
But pride, oh pride, was our favourite treat.

We grew up watching iron turn kind,
Discipline soften a grieving mind.
We saw our mothers hold the line,
When storms broke hearts but love stayed fine.

We learnt that home is not a place,
It's courage wrapped in warm embrace.
It's laughter shared across the miles,
Through army phones and pixel smiles.

Our bonds—like knots on a sturdy rope,
Braided with faith, and stitched with hope.
When one kid leaves, another stays,
Yet somehow, we're woven always.

In every Fauji child's steady gaze,
You'll find the calm of war-time haze.
Strength that bends but never breaks,
A heart that gives more than it takes.

We carry stories few can read,

Of sacrifice that blooms like seed.
Of fathers who missed school parades,
Of mothers who hid their tears in shades.

We're forged in uniforms we never wore,
But felt their weight forevermore.
The anthem runs in every vein,
A gentle pride, a sacred chain.

And though the world may never know,
How deep our quiet rivers flow—
We stand with hearts both wild and wise,
Fauji kids, beneath endless skies.

For we are children of the march and dawn,
Of the flag that waves when hope is gone.
We live, we move, we love, we mend—
In every goodbye, we find a friend.

25. "The Rank Beyond Gender"

In olive green she stands so tall,
A shadow cast on every wall.
Not daughter, wife, or someone's pride—
A soldier first, the rest aside.

She wakes before the break of dawn,
Her courage stitched, her fears long gone.
Steel in her gaze, yet heart so wide,
Where duty lives and dreams reside.

They said, "It's not a woman's fight,"
Yet she marched on through day and night.
Through sweat and storm, through pain and fear,
She earned the stars they said were "dear."

Her hands bear callus, scars, and grit,
Each mark a tale she won't admit.
The world still asks, "But can she cope?"
Her silence answers — carved in hope.

While whispers trail her battle run,
She fights two wars — one by one.
One at the border, fierce and loud,
One in the crowd that doubts her vow.

A soldier's soul knows no divide,
No gender line, no weaker side.
For in her chest, that steady drum,
Beats valour's tune — forever young.

She salutes the flag, her anchor, her guide,
No lipstick, war paint, just honour and pride.
Her march resounds through time and sand,
A thunder that shakes a biased land.

Her uniform — not fit, but faith,
Tailored with sacrifice and wraith.
For blood bleeds red, not pink or blue,
And soldier hood is earned, not due.

When history writes her, let it be clear,
She wasn't "the first" — she was here.
And when her medals catch the light,
They gleam for all who dared the fight.

So, when you see her, head held high,

Salute not her face, but the why —
For she reminds the world once more:
A soldier's spirit knows no shore.

A woman? Yes. A warrior too.
A soldier — wholly, through and through.
The rank she bears, the path she paved —
Not born to follow, born to be brave.

26. "Under His Command - The Olive Chapter"

A new sun rose on the olive land,
Duty called — he took command.
The flag soared high, the bugles cried,
And pride marched on, step for stride.

The air was charged, the ranks aligned,
The past saluted, the future signed.
1881 — the regiment's soul,
Medicine and might, one sacred goal.

My soldier stood — calm, composed,
A leader born, a life reposed.
His eyes, a mirror of storm and steel,
Yet soft within — the heart to heal.

The Commanding Officer — that sacred name,
Not just rank, but a soldier's flame.
Each star on his shoulder, earned, not worn,
Through sleepless nights and fates reborn.

And I beside — his equal part,
The "First Lady" with a Fauji heart.
A silent general of homes and grace,
A smile the balm for every face.

Our home became the beating core,
Of lives entwined through duty's door.
Tea simmered with laughter's blend,
Every guest — a friend, no end.

Mess nights bright with stories told,
Of war and wit, of brave and bold.
The band played tunes of love and fight,
Beneath the stars of cantonment night.

Yet beneath the shine, the charm, the cheer,
Lurks every Fauji wife's silent fear.
The calls at dawn, the knocks at two,
The burden shared, the strength we brew.

For command is not a post of ease,
It's walking storms with practiced peace.
To lead is to feel, to serve, to stand,
To cradle souls in a steady hand.

He walks through tents where pain resides,

Where courage bleeds, yet hope abides.
The medics toil, the gunners roar,
And still, humanity beats at the core.

Between the guns and healing cries,
Faith and fire entwine, arise.
He leads them both — the sword, the salve,
In one great symphony, fierce yet halved.

The perks? They're subtle — not of gold,
But bonds of trust, fierce and bold.
A salute that warms more than the sun,
A bond where many hearts beat as one.

And I — the keeper of this home in green,
Where life is fragile, yet serene.
Between the drills and dinners grand,
We learn what few can understand.

That service is love in its purest tone,
That rank may shine, but hearts alone
Make every post, every march, every stand —
Worth every tear, under His Command.

27. "Come What May, Life Goes On"

From morning light to evening grey,
We learn to live, come what may.
A child wakes up, shoes untied,
Spills the milk, then wants to hide.
A scraped knee, a tearful plea,
Yet finds the strength to climb the tree.

Adolescents fight the inner storm,
The pressure builds to fit the norm.
Tests, exams, first crush's pain,
Learning heartbreak is part of the gain.
They stumble, fall, yet rise anew,
Discovering dreams they can pursue.

Young adults rush through work and pay,
Bills to settle, debts to sway.
Coffee spills, missed deadlines stress,
Yet laughter breaks the heaviness.
Friendships strain, romances bend,

Lessons linger, hearts will mend.

Family life with children, chores,
Life feels heavy, endless chores.
Late-night cries, burnt toast at ten,
Arguments with wife and then—
A smile, a hug, a small delight,
Turns chaos into quiet light.

Midlife hits with sudden fear,
Health complaints, a fleeting year.
Dreams deferred, ambitions stalled,
The mirror shows a life recalled.
Yet learning now to slow the pace,
Finding joy in simple space.

Old age comes with aching knees,
Memories like autumn leaves.
Grandchildren laugh, the world spins by,
Stories told beneath the sky.
Regrets may whisper, losses weigh,
Yet peace arrives—come what may.

Through all the struggles, small or vast,
We grow, we falter, yet we last.
The heart that bends, the soul that fights,
Finds beauty even in darkest nights.

So, rise each morning, face the fray,
Live, love, endure—come what may.

28. "Crimson Veil : The Tale Of Sindoor"

When dusk fell silent over the rugged land,
And whispers of danger swept like sand,
The nation shivered in its restless sleep,
Yet heroes stirred where shadows creep.

Through valleys shrouded in the midnight mist,
Came boots that knew no fear, no tryst,
Their hearts beat the drum of a soldier's vow,
To shield the motherland then and now.

Operation Sindoor—its name whispered strong,
A call to right what had been wrong.
Not for glory, not for fleeting fame,
But to etch in history a nation's claim.

In the hush of night, the engines roared,
The brave moved forward, the borders explored.
Each step measured, each breath a prayer,
For the land they loved, and those who dare.

Rivers ran red in metaphor alone,
Yet courage shone, the steel of bone.
Politics murmured from distant halls,
But valour answers when the duty calls.

Through ambush, storm, and treacherous height,
Through endless hours of relentless fight,
The soldier knows no party, creed, or name,
Only the flag, the flame, the eternal aim.

From trenches deep to the mountain's crest,
Every heartbeat pledged to the motherland's quest.
Families trembled in whispered fear,
Yet the army's resolve made safety near.

When all seemed lost, when hope was thin,
The lion's roar came from deep within.
Operation Sindoor—etched in the scroll of time,
A symphony of grit, in rhythm and rhyme.

For politics may falter, and debates may tear,
But a soldier stands, beyond all care.
Crimson duty, honour's core,
A nation sleeps, yet fears no more.

So, sing, O winds, of courage untold,

Of hearts unbroken, and spirits bold.
**Operation Sindoor, a saga of might,
Where shadow met valour, and dark met light.**

29. "Once a Soldier, Always a Soldier"
(An Ode to Those Who Never Stop Serving)

The uniform is folded, the medals sleep,
But the soldier's promise runs bone-deep.
No war outside, yet wars within,
No orders shouted—still, they begin.

At dawn, they rise—no bugle calls,
Just birds that march across the walls.
Tea in hand, the mission clear:
"Hold the fort, protect those dear."

They walk the home like sacred ground,
Each corner mapped, each noise profound.
Old instincts hum beneath their skin—
They check the locks, then check again.

The neighbours smile, they never know,
This calm comes from surviving snow.
From standing guard when hope was thin,
From losing friends—and holding in.

They miss the barrack's bantering din,
That chaos sweet, that steel within.
The muddy jokes, the midnight tea,
The mad, unmatched fraternity.

Now life's a battle, soft but strange,
Where peace feels like a field exchange.
The children giggle, "Papa's odd!"
While he salutes their cereal squad.

The spouse just sighs—half love, half laugh,
When they plan groceries like a staff.
"Target bread aisle, left flank clear—
We move at sharp 0900, dear."

Civilians—they don't quite get,
Why soldiers never just forget.
Why eyes still scan, why steps still fall,
In silent rhythm, through it all.

They call them proud, perhaps unkind,
A bit too stiff, a bit out of mind.

But arrogance? No—just grace in scars,
And discipline written in the stars.

Their heart still hums that marching song,
Even when days feel dull or wrong.
Their wars are softer now—of care,
Of fixing toys, of saying prayer.

Yet deep inside, that fire stays,
That oath, that code, that soldier's blaze.
For every bruise, for every loss,
They still salute what life will toss.

And when the anthem fills the air,
They stand—no thought, just being there.
Because the world may change its tune,
But their spirit still guards the moon.

Home is now their base command,
The world they rule with steady hand.
From laundry drills to bedtime calls,
They serve with pride—no borders, no walls.

So laugh if you will, but bow in heart,
To those who mastered both war and art.
For peace is not their easy grace—
It's courage—lived in every space.

Once a soldier, always so,
Through quiet dawns and sunsets' glow.
They've traded guns for love's control—
But the uniform still fits the soul.

30. "March Of The Eternal Guard"
The Unyielding Saga Of The Indian Army

From Himalayan heights where the cold winds scream,
To deserts ablaze under the sun's fiery gleam,
From riverbeds that run with a thousand tales,
To storm-tossed seas and relentless gales—
They move, they march, with resolve unbroken,
Every step a vow, every word unspoken.

Through valleys shrouded in shadowed fear,
Through nights when silence presses near,
They stride with hearts that never yield,
Their courage sharp, their honour a shield.
Not a backward glance, not a faltering breath,
They rise, they fight, they conquer death.

The drums of destiny beat in their chest,

For the soil they guard is never at rest.
From the first light of dawn to twilight's fall,
Their march echoes the motherland's call.
Every ridge, every fort, every jagged stone,
Holds stories of valour etched in bone.

Forward, always forward—their eternal creed,
Through trials that crush, through wounds that bleed.
Steel in hand, fire in soul,
Every battle fought makes the nation whole.
No fear can bind, no shadow restrain,
For they rise through darkness, again and again.

See them scale cliffs where the eagle's nest,
Cross rivers raging, brave every test.
Through storms, through smoke, through hunger and pain,
They endure, they persevere, they rise again.
Their eyes hold the glint of a thousand suns,
A promise unbroken, a war never done.

O land of the brave, behold their might,
In the longest day and the darkest night.
Every salute, every flag held high,
Is a hymn to the valour that will never die.
Forward ever, backward never, their song,
A legacy eternal, timeless and strong.

And when the world falters, when hope seems dim,
They march in silence, undaunted, grim.
For the soldier knows, above all things,
The honour of duty is the crown he brings.
To nation, to people, to earth and sky,
They move like thunder—relentless, nigh.

So let the mountains echo, let rivers proclaim,
The Indian Army forever, immortal in name.
Through ages, through storms, through history's tide,
They are the shield, the heart, the nation's pride.
Ever forward, their spirits soar,
An eternal saga, now and forevermore.

www.ingramcontent.com/pod-product-compliance
Lightning Source LLC
Chambersburg PA
CBHW060210050426
42446CB00013B/3041

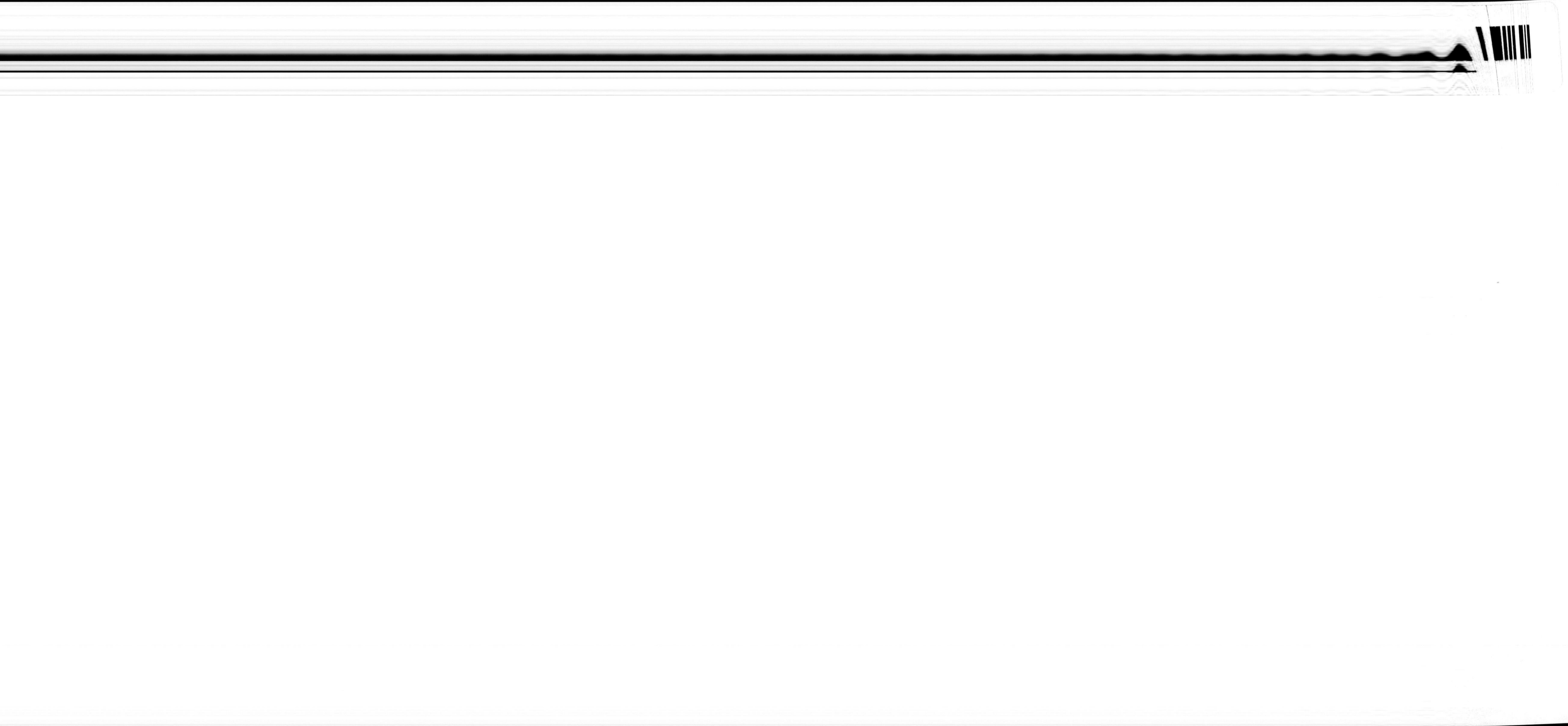

www.ingramcontent.com/pod-product-compliance
Lightning Source LLC
Chambersburg PA
CBHW060210050426
42446CB00013B/3041